NEW YORK
LANDMARKS

*A Collection of Architecture
and Historical Details*

Photography & Text by
Charles J. Ziga

**BARNES
&NOBLE
BOOKS**
NEW YORK

"Give me your tired, your poor,
Your huddled masses yearning to breathe free,
The wretched refuse of your teeming shore,
Send these, the homeless, tempest-tossed to me:
I lift my lamp beside the golden door."

From
THE NEW COLOSSUS
EMMA LAZARUS, 1883

For Annie

NEW YORK LANDMARKS

Contents

City Hall	4
Schermerhorn Row	6
Federal Hall National Memorial	8
Trinity Church and Churchyard	10
Brooklyn Bridge	12
Saint Patrick's Cathedral	14
Dakota Apartments	16
Statue of Liberty	18
Central Park	20
Carnegie Hall	22
Washington Memorial Arch	24
Immigrant Receiving Station	26
Flatiron Building	28
Macy's	30
New York Stock Exchange	32
Battery Park Control House	34
Times Square	36
Plaza Hotel	38
New York Public Library	40
Woolworth Building	42
Grand Central Terminal	44
Metropolitan Museum of Art	46
Chrysler Building	48
Empire State Building	50
Rockefeller Center	52
Radio City Music Hall	54
United Nations	56
Solomon R. Guggenheim Museum	58
Lincoln Center for the Performing Arts	60
World Trade Center	62
Bibliography	64

CITY HALL
New York's architectural treasure

CITY HALL PARK, BETWEEN BROADWAY AND PARK ROW

City Hall, completed in 1811, continues to house the Mayor's office and City Council Chambers. It is New York's welcoming center for important dignitaries, returning soldiers, celebrities, athletes and astronauts. This elegant scaled-down palace combines the *Federal* style with *French Renaissance* details. The building is situated in City Hall Park, the town green of the city. Since colonial times, the park has been the site of parades, protests, riots and celebrations.

Joseph F. Mangin and **John McComb,** *Architects.* Awarded the commission by their competition-winning design. McComb is attributed with the *Georgian* style interior and Mangin, a French émigré, with the elegant *French Renaissance* details and graceful ornamentation of the exterior.

The two-story building is symmetrical with a one-story central portico and projecting wings. The façade's rows of arched windows are decorated with Corinthian pilasters to each side and swags above. The building was originally finished in white marble with base and north façade of New Jersey brownstone. One hundred and ninety years ago City Hall was at the northern edge of New York City, and therefore the northern side was clad in brownstone in order to save money. By 1895, the building had fallen into terrible disrepair and was threatened by demolition. Because of public outcry, renovations have since occurred, the last being in 1956 when the exterior, including the north side, was refinished in Alabama limestone. The clock in the cupola was added in 1831 and was the first illuminated clock in New York City. A figure of *Justice,* designed by John Dixey, crowns the cupola.

The interior is classic *Georgian.* At the central rotunda is a sweeping pair of self-supporting marble stairs. On the second floor of the rotunda ten Corinthian columns support a coffered dome with a glass oculus.

N.Y.C. Landmark February 1, 1966.

SCHERMERHORN ROW

Street of ships

FULTON STREET, AT THE SOUTH STREET SEAPORT

Built between 1811–12, in the *Georgian-Federal* tradition of architecture, Schermerhorn Row was one of the earliest commercial developments in New York. When the area was a major shipping center its 12 buildings housed chandleries (selling provisions for ships), sail lofts, rope lofts and naval store warehouses.

Peter Schermerhorn, *Merchant and Ship Owner.* Constructed these buildings to lease to sailing merchants. Schermerhorn operated his own prosperous ship chandlery from 243 Water Street.

The four-story row houses on Fulton Street, Front Street and South Street were built on land-filled water lots (land between extremes of high and low tides). Red Flemish bond brickwork, plain stone lintels, arched entrances of brownstone, tall brick chimneys and steep Georgian hip roofs of slate are the buildings' original features. The area became a busy commercial district in 1816, when the Brooklyn Ferry put a landing at Schermerhorn's wharf. Soon after, the Fulton Market opened across the street. In the late 1800s dormers and *Greek Revival* style cast iron storefronts were added to the building to serve ships' passengers. In 1868, the building on the corner of South and Fulton Streets was converted into a hotel. The fifth story and the mansard roof with dormers were added for additional rooms.

In 1968 Schermerhorn Row was protected by the New York City Landmarks Commission and became an integral part of the South Street Seaport Historical District. It was restored in 1983 by Jan Hird Pokorny and Cabrera & Barricklo, Architects.

N.Y.C. Landmark October 29, 1968.

FEDERAL HALL NATIONAL MEMORIAL

Site of the first capitol of the United States

28 WALL STREET

Federal Hall National Memorial is situated on one of New York's most historic sites. Here once stood New York City's first City Hall (later called Federal Hall) where the first U. S. Congress met and where George Washington took his oath as the first President of the United States in 1789. In 1812 the original building was demolished and sold as salvage for $425. The current building, constructed 1834–42, was originally a U. S. Custom House. It later became a U. S. Sub-Treasury and, in 1939, a National Monument under the National Parks Service. Today, the building serves as a museum for American and New York history.

Ithiel Town and **Alexander Jackson Davis,** *Architects.* Awarded the commission based on their *Greek Revival* design.

Samuel Thompson, *Construction Architect.* **John Frazee,** *Interior Architect.*

The ideals of Greek democracy and Roman republicanism that influenced the Founding Fathers were reflected in their choice of classical architecture for public buildings. The classic Greek temple rests on a high plinth with a steep flight of steps. A portico with 32-foot-high Doric columns supports a simple pediment without ornamentation.

The interior rotunda is dominated by a paneled dome (not a typical Greek form) that is 60 feet in diameter and which is supported by 16 two-story-high Corinthian columns. The rich ornate Roman interior is a contrast to the simple Greek exterior.

The statue of *George Washington* is by J. Q. A. Ward, 1883.

National Landmark 1939. N.Y.C. Landmark December 21, 1965.

TRINITY CHURCH AND CHURCHYARD

A green oasis amid the concrete
BROADWAY AT WALL STREET

C ompleted in 1846, after seven years of construction, Trinity Church served the first Episcopalian parish in New York and was the tallest building in the area until the late 1860s.

Richard Upjohn, *Architect.* English-American. Founder of the American Institute of Architects and its first President, 1857–76.

Richard Morris Hunt, *Architect.* Designed the six sculptured bronze doors illustrating biblical scenes and the history of Trinity Church. The bas-relief detail (inset) represents Revelation VI, verses 15, 16 and 17. Like Upjohn, Hunt was a founder of the American Institute of Architects.

The *Gothic Revival* church, 79 feet wide and 166 feet long, is built of New Jersey brownstone and has flying buttresses, stained glass windows, Gothic tracery and medieval sculptures. Located at the head of Wall Street, the central tower with octagonal spire and cross measures 280 ½ feet tall. Its bells were imported from London in 1797 and are the oldest in New York. Trinity Church is the third church to be built on the site. King William III of England gave the land to the church in 1697 and the original church, completed a year later, was burned in the Great Fire of 1776. The second church was demolished in 1839 after structural failure.

Trinity Churchyard, established even before the first church (the oldest gravestone dates from 1681), includes graves and memorials of historical New Yorkers such as Francis Lewis (signer of the Declaration of Independence), Alexander Hamilton (Secretary of the U. S. Treasury), William Bradford (founder of the city's first newspaper, the *Gazette*) and Robert Fulton (inventor). It remains one of the last green sites in the Financial District.

N.Y.C. Landmark August 16, 1966.

BROOKLYN BRIDGE

World's first steel-wire suspension bridge

MANHATTAN (CITY HALL PARK) TO BROOKLYN (CADMAN PLAZA)

On May 24, 1883, after 13 years of construction, the Brooklyn Bridge became the first bridge to span the East River, uniting the boroughs of Brooklyn and Manhattan. The bridge's construction cost was over $16 million. It remained the largest bridge in the world until 1903, when the Williamsburg Bridge (4½ ft. longer) was completed.

John A. Roebling, *Engineer.* An immigrant from Prussia and designer of the bridge. While directing the bridge's surveying he was injured in an accident and died before construction began.

Colonel Washington A. Roebling. Became the *Chief Construction Engineer* after his father's death.

With its two *Gothic* towers rising 276 feet, the bridge was the second highest structure in New York in 1883. Only the Trinity Church spire was taller. Its four main cables made of steel-wires were a first in bridge construction. Each cable, 15¾ inches in diameter, contains 5,434 wires and is 3,515 feet long. The bridge stretches 5,989 feet long overall, with a center span of 1,595½ feet between its two towers, and is 85 feet wide.

A grand celebration with fireworks opened the bridge in 1883. One week later, twelve pedestrians were trampled to death on the bridge's promenade when the crowd thought the bridge was collapsing and panicked.

The Brooklyn Bridge has been a source of inspiration to many U. S. artists, including Walt Whitman, Hart Crane, Thomas Wolfe, John Marin and Joseph Stella. The bridge's 100th birthday was celebrated in 1983.

N.Y.C. Landmark August 24, 1967.

SAINT PATRICK'S CATHEDRAL

Dedicated to the patron saint of Ireland

FIFTH AVENUE, BETWEEN 50TH AND 51ST STREETS

Saint Patrick's is the largest Roman Catholic church in the U.S. and the seat of the Archdiocese of New York. The cathedral took 21 years to build: four times longer and at twice the cost estimated. Cardinal John McCloskey formally blessed and opened the cathedral on May 25, 1879. The spires were completed nine years later and the Lady Chapel was added in 1906.

Archbishop John Hughes, *First Catholic Archbishop of New York.* Irish immigrant. The building of Saint Patrick's as a branch to Saint Patrick's cathedral on Prince Street was his original idea.

James Renwick, Jr., *Architect.* Renwick also designed the Smithsonian Institution in Washington, D.C.

Originally the land was intended for a burial ground, but it was too rocky. When the cathedral was constructed, it rested on the very outskirts of the city and its spires dominated the surrounding skyline until the 1930s. Today, it is dwarfed by the glass and steel skyscrapers of midtown Manhattan.

The *French Gothic* cathedral, 174 feet wide x 332 feet long, is the eleventh largest church in the world. Constructed of white marble, it is in the shape of a Latin cross with traditional east-west orientation. Above the central entrance is a circular rose window, 26 feet in diameter and to each side, a foliated tracery spire rises 330 feet high. The north tower holds the cathedral's chimes of 19 bells. Three sets of bronze doors, designed by Charles Maginnis and John Angel in 1949, comprise the cathedral's formal entrances. The bas-relief detail from the central doors (inset) represents Elizabeth Ann Seton, the first American-born saint.

The nave (central seating area) is 108 feet high and 48 feet wide. Forming the cathedral's focal point is the sanctuary with its 57-foot-high bronze baldachin.

N.Y.C. Landmark October 19, 1966.

DAKOTA APARTMENTS

It might as well be in the Dakota Territory

72ND STREET AND CENTRAL PARK WEST

The city's first luxury apartment house was named after the Indian region in the northwestern U. S. because it was located so far from the city's center. At the time of its completion in 1884, the building was surrounded by vacant land and squatters' shacks. Early Dakota residents had views of the incompleted Central Park, Long Island Sound, the hills of Brooklyn and the Hudson River.

Edward S. Clark, *Singer Sewing Machine Heir, Developer.* He turned people's mocking of the building's location into its namesake. Western ornamentations of arrowheads, sheaves of wheat and an Indian head relief (inset) are incorporated into the building's design.

Henry J. Hardenbergh, *Architect.* Also designer of the Plaza Hotel.

Reminiscent of a château, the eight-story yellow brick mass is articulated by brownstone and terra cotta gables, bay windows, recessed and projecting balconies, cornices, trim and ornamentation. The steep pitched slate roof is adorned with chimneys, dormers and copper cresting. Surrounding the building is an iron-fenced moat with sea monsters and masks of Zeus.

The main entrance, a two-story arched gateway on 72nd Street, leads into a inner courtyard with two fountains. At each of the courtyard's four corners is an entrance and elevator. There were originally 85 apartments, each with 4-5 rooms (a typical living room measures 25 ft. x 40 ft.) with 12-15-foot ceilings and wood burning fireplaces. The interiors were finished in mahogany and oak with marble mantles and brass fixtures. Walls two feet thick and 18-inch thick-floors make it one of the quietest buildings in the city. Originally, the Dakota housed its own electrical generator because the city's electrical system had not reached that far north.

Famous tenants of the Dakota, past and present, include: Boris Karloff, Lauren Bacall, Leonard Bernstein, Roberta Flack and John Lennon.

N.Y.C. Landmark, February 11, 1969.

STATUE OF LIBERTY
Liberty Enlightening the World
LIBERTY ISLAND (BEDLOE'S ISLAND), NEW YORK HARBOR

France presented the statue on July 4, 1884 as a gift from the French people to the American people. The statue took 11 years to build at a cost of $400,000 and was dedicated on Bedloe's Island on October 28, 1886.

Édouard-René Lefebvre de Laboulaye, *French Historian.* Paris, France. Credited with the idea of a statue symbolizing the joining of France and the United States in the common quest for liberty and freedom.

Frédéric-Auguste Bartholdi, *Sculptor.* Paris, France. The statue was caricatured after his mother and Delacroix's painting *Liberty Leading the People to the Barricades.*

Alexandre Gustave Eiffel, *Engineer.* Paris, France. Engineered the statue's internal iron and steel skeletal frame. He also designed the Eiffel Tower.

Richard Morris Hunt, *Architect.* Designed the statue's 154-foot-high pedestal of Stony Creek granite and concrete. The funds for the pedestal were raised publically in the United States.

The statue, which stands 151 feet tall, is made of 300 copper sheets rivetted to and supported by a steel and iron framework. Her crown interior can accommodate up to 30 people. The length of her right arm with torch is 45 feet. Copper oxidizing gives the statue her green color (patina).

Broken shackles at Liberty's feet signify escape from tyranny; the 21-foot torch symbolizes light of truth and justice illuminating the world; the spikes of her crown denote the sun's rays enlightening the world; the tablet date represents the Declaration of Independence: July 4, 1776. After being renovated by Richard S. Hayden and Thierry W. Despont, Architects, 1984–86, she was rededicated on October 28, 1986 for her 100th birthday.

National Monument 1924. N.Y.C. Landmark September 14, 1976.

CENTRAL PARK

New York's emerald treasure

59TH STREET TO 110TH STREET, FIFTH AVENUE TO EIGHTH AVENUE

Central Park, the first planned public park in the United States, is one of New York's, indeed the country's, finest treasures. Since 1857, the park has continued to evolve, meeting the changes of society, yet still adhering to Olmsted's and Vaux's original design intent.

William Cullen Bryant, *Editor of the N.Y. Evening Post* and **Andrew Jackson Downing,** *Landscape Architect and Publisher of the Horticulturist* were instrumental in gathering support for a large public park in New York City.

Frederick Law Olmsted, *Engineer and Landscape Architect,* and **Calvert Vaux,** *Architect.* Won the competition and the $2,000 award with their **Greensward Plan.** Their design integrated architecture with land-scaping to accommodate the uneven typography.

The 840-acre park is 2½ miles long and ½ mile wide and located in the heart of Manhattan Island. The park's southern half is more pastoral with open landscape and its northern half is more rugged with wooded landscape. Foot paths, bridal paths, curved carriage drives (to discourage carriage racing) and four sunken transverse roads provide for pedestrian and motor traffic. The 36 arched bridges which grace the park were all designed by Calvert Vaux and each is different. During construction, over 4 million trees (632 species) and 815 varieties of vines, plants and flowers were planted, and over 10 million cartloads of dirt were moved.

The park's major points of interest are the Bethesda Fountain at the Terrace (inset), Belvedere Castle, the Mall, Delacorte Theater, Strawberry Fields, Wollman Memorial Rink, the Conservatory Garden and the Zoo.

N.Y.C. Scenic Landmark April 16, 1974. National Historical Landmark 1935.

CARNEGIE HALL

How do you get to Carnegie Hall? — Practice, practice, practice

57TH STREET AND SEVENTH AVENUE

Carnegie Hall (formerly Music Hall) opened May 5, 1891 with the American premiere performance of Peter Ilyich Tchaikovsky conducting his *Marche Solennelle*. Since then, it has become a world renowned concert hall, more famous for its near perfect acoustics than its architecture.

Andrew Carnegie, *Steel Magnate, Philanthropist.* A Scottish immigrant, he donated $2 million to build the concert hall through the urging of **Walter Damrosch,** Conductor of the Oratorio Society of New York and the New York Symphony Society.

William Burnet Tuthill, *Architect.* His research of European concert halls and the technology available 100 years ago resulted in the outstanding acoustics of Carnegie Hall.

The hall has been host to the world's greatest conductors, musicians and performers including Toscanini, Bernstein, Ella Fitzgerald, Charlie Parker, the Rolling Stones and the Beatles. In addition it has served as a lecture hall for such notables as Martin Luther King, Jr., Winston Churchill, Eleanor Roosevelt and Mark Twain. In the 1960s, Isaac Stern, violinist, gathered support to save Carnegie Hall from demolition.

The famous acoustics are attributed to the soft curved planes of the balconies and the elliptical ceiling which allows sound to bounce fractured, at small angles, around the hall. The velvet adorning the hall helps to absorb the reverberation and echoes.

The modest exterior is made of pale brown Roman bricks with Roman arches, pilasters, and terra cotta ornamentation. The building's original mansard roof was replaced by a sixth floor of studios. Carnegie Hall is an early example of a mixed-use building with offices, studios, shops, theater, recital hall and concert hall.

N.Y.C. Landmark June 20, 1967.

WASHINGTON MEMORIAL ARCH

Exitus acta probat

WASHINGTON SQUARE NORTH AT FIFTH AVENUE

In 1889, a temporary wood and stucco arch was built to commemorate the centennial anniversary of the inauguration of George Washington as the first president of the United States. It was so well received that the current memorial arch was built in 1892 and dedicated on April 30, 1895.

William Rhinelander Stewart. Credited with the arch's concept and for raising the funds, $2,765, from the Washington Square residents.

Stanford White, of McKim, Mead & White, *Architect.* Designed both the wood and stucco arch and the marble arch.

Rising at the foot of Fifth Avenue, the white marble triumphal arch (77 ft. H x 30ft. W x 10ft. D) dominates the northern entrance to Washington Square Park. Two winged figures of Victory in relief are carved above the 47-foot-high arch. Emblems of war and peace adorn the columns and a sculptured American Eagle, large decorative stars and Ws decorate the frieze.

The sculpture on the west pier is *Washington in Peace* with *Justice* and *Wisdom* (inset). The inscribed Latin (*Exitus acta probat*) in the book behind Washington means "The end justifies the deed." The sculpture was created by Alexander Stirling Calder, father of Alexander Calder (the sculptor of mobiles). On the East pier can be found *Washington in War* with *Fame* and *Valor*, by Herman A. MacNeil. Unfortunately, the marble statuary is deteriorating from the city's pollution.

Washington Square Park was constructed in 1827 and soon afterward the area became a wealthy residential area. In 1837, New York University began erecting its first building on the east side of the park. Now, many of the university's buildings are within the park's vicinity.

N.Y.C. Historical District April 29, 1969.

IMMIGRANT RECEIVING STATION

First steps in a new land

ELLIS ISLAND, NEW YORK HARBOR

The original Ellis Island Immigrant Receiving Station opened its doors to the first immigrant, Annie Moore of Cork, Ireland, in 1892. Five years later it was destroyed by fire. The current building, built in the *French Renaissance* style, cost $1.5 million. On December 17, 1900, its first day of operations, 2,251 immigrants were processed. The building remained the nation's primary immigration reception depot until 1924. Only two percent of the 16 million or more immigrants who had passed through its doors were sent back to their countries of origin. Its peak year was 1907, when 1.2 million immigrants came through Ellis Island. The station closed as an immigration center in 1954. The building has also served as a Coast Guard Station and an enemy alien detention center.

William A. Boring and **Edward L. Tilton,** *Architects.*

The Immigrant Receiving Station (the principle structure on Ellis Island) is constructed of heavily rusticated limestone and red brick with limestone ornamentation. Between the three colossal arches of the entry are two limestone American Eagle statues. Rising up from the four corners of the central pavilion are four 134-foot-high copper-capped towers. Inside on the second floor is the building's grandest room, Registry Hall. Its 50-foot vaulted ceiling is adorned with interlocking terra-cotta tiles. Other buildings in this complex include the hospital, powerhouse, dormitories and dining hall. The island itself grew from a sand bar to its current 27 acre site primarily from dirt excavated from construction of the New York subway system.

In 1984 the building was closed for renovation and restoration under the direction of Beyer, Blinder & Belle/Notter Finegold & Alexander, and reopened as a National Museum in September, 1990.

National Historic Landmark, May 11, 1965.

FLATIRON BUILDING
Twenty-three skidoo

The Flatiron Building derives its name from its triangular shape created by the intersection of Broadway and Fifth Avenue at 23rd Street. It was the world's tallest building when it was completed in 1902, marking the beginnings of the skyscraper era in New York City.

Daniel H. Burnham of D. H. Burnham & Co., *Architect.* Chicago. Burnham also designed one of the earliest skyscrapers, the Monadnock Building in Chicago, 1891.

Covering the entire lot, the 21-story, 285-foot-high building extends in an unbroken mass without any setbacks. The steel framework is clad with rusticated limestone and molded terra cotta in *Renaissance Revival* style. The vertical composition is the classic tripart, based on the divisions of a column (base, shaft and capitol top). The base (first four floors) is heavily rusticated, giving the building a solid anchor. The ornate capitol, with two-story arches and an enormous cornice, provides a visual stop to the continuous twelve-story shaft.

In the early 1900s strong down drafts from the building created a spectacle of young ladies' long skirts being lifted, exposing their ankles. Reputedly, their admirers were cleared away with shouts of "Twenty-three skidoo" from the policemen directing traffic.

Originally known as the Fuller Building after its developer, its name changed through public perceptions. Viewed from uptown on Fifth Avenue, the building has been compared to the bow of a ship. Its rounded apex at 23rd Street is only six feet across.

N.Y.C. Landmark September 20, 1966.

MACY*S

The world's largest store

34TH STREET FROM BROADWAY TO SEVENTH AVENUE

As the world's largest store, Macy's boasts over two million square feet of floor space. Its 300 selling departments stock over a half-million different items. For over 130 years Macy's has served as one of the city's leading retail establishments.

Rowland Hussey Macy, *Nantucket Whaling Captain, Merchant.* Started Macy's in 1858 at Sixth Avenue and 14th Street. The Macy's red star logo was based on a tattoo he had on his hand from his younger days as a Nantucket whaler.

Isidor and **Nathan Straus,** *Merchants.* Originally leasing the rights to the store's glass, china and silver departments, they took controlling interest in Macy's after Rowland Macy's death and moved the store to its current location at 34th and Broadway in 1902.

De Lemos & Cordes, *Architects.* Designed the original Broadway building.

Robert D. Kohn, *Architect.* Designed the Seventh Avenue addition.

Macy's department store actually consists of two buildings; the Broadway side is the original building and the Seventh Avenue side was added in 1931. The nine-story building (200 ft.W x 700 ft.L) is constructed of red brick and limestone. On the Broadway façade, the middle floors are articulated vertically with superimposed bay windows and four-story high Corinthian columns. Above the bay windows are *Palladian* style arched windows.

The four caryatids (columns shaped like women) on the 34th Street façade entrance are by J. Massey Rhind. Other original details on the 34th Street façade include the canopy, clock and turn-of-the century Macy's lettering.

The main selling floor has been restored to reveal the 1930s *Art Deco* style.

New York Stock Exchange

The big board

8 Broad Street

Completed in 1903, this building houses one of the most important financial institutions in the United States.

The **Buttonwood Agreement** (May 17, 1792) is the original document drafted by 24 brokers to form the *New York Stock Exchange Board.* It was named after the buttonwood (sycamore) tree under which their trading of bonds began. A buttonwood tree was planted outside the entrance at 20 Wall Street to commemorate the organization's origins.

George B. Post, *Architect.* Awarded the commission by his competition-winning design.

The *Greek Revival* building has a rusticated two-story base with rectangular and rounded arched openings. On the base are six 52-foot-high Corinthian columns which support a classic Greek pediment. Behind the columns is a four-story glass curtain wall admitting light into the trading room, which has marble walls and a gilded ceiling.

The statuary in the pediment, *Integrity Protecting the Works of Man,* was designed by J. Q. A. Ward and Paul Bartlett. The statuary includes: *Integrity,* center, *Agriculture* and *Mining* on her left and *Science, Industry* and *Invention* on her right. The original marble statuary was destroyed by the city's pollution and replaced by copper and lead figures, coated to resemble stone in 1936.

The New York Stock Exchange Board has 1,366 members. There are over 1,700 leading companies with more than 5,000 stock and bond offerings listed on the exchange. The price of a seat on the Stock Exchange fluctuates; in 1929, a seat sold for as much as $625,000, ten years later the top price paid was $85,000, and in 1990 the top price was $450,000.

N.Y.C. Landmark July 9, 1985.

BATTERY PARK CONTROL HOUSE

5¢ Fare — 1904–1947

BOWLING GREEN SUBWAY STATION, LEXINGTON AVENUE IRT

The Battery Park Control House is one of the last three remaining kiosks of the city's first subway line, the Interborough Rapid Transit Corporation (IRT) which began service on October 27, 1904. It was the original access to the Bowling Green Station.

George L. Heins and **Christopher La Farge,** *Architects.* Many of the IRT's original kiosks and subway details were of their design. They were also the first architects of the Cathedral of St. John the Divine.

John B. McDonald, *Construction Contractor.*

August Belmont, *Financier and First President of the IRT.*

The Control House derives its name from the idea that once passengers entered the building they were under control of the subway company. The building is yellow brick with limestone cornerstones and a granite base. The gabled ends are decorated with a limestone bulls-eye and a clock.

Subway stations throughout New York feature decorative mosaics and moldings dating from the turn of the century. The steamboat relief from Fulton Station (inset), portrays Robert Fulton's first steamboat, the Clairmont.

New York was also serviced by two other subway lines, the Brooklyn-Manhattan Transit Corp. (BMT) and the Eighth Avenue (Independent), which had their own routes, tracks and stations. Each were once privately owned, but are now united under the New York City Transit Authority, the most comprehensive subway system in the world. The subway carries 3.5 million passengers a day over its 722 miles of track to a total of 469 subway stations in Manhattan, Brooklyn, Queens and the Bronx.

N.Y.C. Landmark November 20, 1973.

TIMES SQUARE

Crossroads of the world

42ND STREET AT SEVENTH AVENUE AND BROADWAY

Times Square is a triangular area created by the intersection of Seventh Avenue and Broadway at 42nd Street. During the late 1800s, the area was the center for carriage shops and stables, and called Long Acre Square after a similar area in London. In 1904, the square was renamed Times Square in honor of Adolph Ochs' Times Building, home of *The New York Times* daily newspaper. The first theater in the area, the Metropolitan Opera House at Broadway and 40th Street, opened in 1893 and the theater district was born.

"The Great White Way," was a term supposedly coined in 1901 by O. J. Gude, an ad man, describing the possibilities of electric signs for advertising. In the 1920s, when movie palaces began to dominate the area, the electric displays grew to a grand scale. Elaborate signboards, including a cascading waterfall, giant cigarette smoke rings and monstrous neon tumbling peanuts, helped create the Times Square visual mystique. By the 1970s many of the movie palaces had been replaced by glass office skyscrapers and in between these office buildings, pornography found a home. Currently, the Times Square District is undergoing a new building boom with the intent to restore some of the square's past visual excitement.

The world's first moving electric sign was installed on the Times Building in 1928. The 5-foot-high, 360-foot-long ribbon of 14,800 electric lights displays a traveling message around the building. After several years of darkness, the "motograph" was restored and reilluminated in 1986. It displays up-to-the-minute news flashes from the *New York Newsday* newspaper.

Times Square's first New Year's Eve celebration, complete with fireworks, took place on December 31, 1904 when *The New York Times* moved its printing presses into the Times Building. It has remained an annual New Year's Eve tradition, complete with a falling electric ball.

At the northern end of the square stands a statue of American showman George *"Give my regards to Broadway"* M. Cohan, by George Lober (inset).

PLAZA HOTEL
A grand hotel de luxe

FIFTH AVENUE AND CENTRAL PARK SOUTH (59TH STREET)

The magnificent landmark hotel opened on October 1, 1907. The 18-story, 800-room, *French Renaissance* building cost a total of $12.5 million to erect.

Henry J. Hardenbergh, *Architect.* Also designer of the Dakota Apartments.

The hotel's first guest was Alfred G. Vanderbilt, son of Cornelius Vanderbilt, and it has since been host to many famous guests and to society's parties and balls. The Plaza's most infamous and pugnacious guest, a fictitious child of six who lives at the hotel, was created by author Kay Thompson, in her book *Eloise.* A portrait of Eloise hangs in the lobby.

The grand vistas, north to Central Park and east to Grand Army Plaza, affords the hotel one of the most prestigious sites in the city. Its exterior consists of a three-story marble base with a ten-story middle of white brick, capped off by balustrade balconies, a massive cornice and a five-story mansard slate roof with dormers, gables and crested green copper. Two of its corners are rounded and topped with towers. Flags flying from the Fifth Avenue façade represent countries of important foreign guests and dignitaries. The Plaza's insignia, two Ps back to back in a crest, detail the building's ornamentation. The inset above is a lamp post detail.

On the first floor can be found the famous Oak Bar, with its murals depicting scenes from around the Plaza, painted by Everett Shinn; and the Palm Court, with its imported Italian caryatids representing the four seasons.

The Plaza has been the quintessential New York hotel for films including *The Great Gatsby, Plaza Suite* and *Author.* In 1907 the Plaza's most expensive room was $25 a night. Today its least expensive room is $175 a night. The hotel's Presidential Suite can cost as much as $15,000 a night. It comes complete with butler, maid, chef, and Rolls-Royce with chauffeur.

N.Y.C. Landmark December 9, 1969.

NEW YORK PUBLIC LIBRARY

Reading between the lions

FIFTH AVENUE AND WEST 42ND STREET

This building is considered one of the finest examples of *Beaux-Arts* style architecture in America. The library was the result of a merger between the Astor and Lenox Libraries and the Tilden Trust and was constructed on the former Croton Aqueduct Distributing Reservoir. The library opened on May 24, 1911.

John M. Carrère and **Thomas Hastings,** *Architects.* Awarded the commission based upon their competition-winning design.

Dr. John Shaw Billings, *First Director of the Library.* Credited with conceiving the library's basic plan. The Main Reading Room (297 ft. x 78 ft.) was one of Billings' suggestions.

The symmetrical Fifth Avenue façade, constructed of Vermont white marble, sits at the top of a broad flight of steps with expansive terraces on both sides. Three arched bays flanked by paired Corinthian columns form the main entrance. The wings have two-story-high engaged Corinthian columns. Between the columns are arched windows with sculpted lion's mask keystones. A bay with pediments and sculpture completes each end of the building. The building is lavishly ornate, both inside and out with sculptured lions, cherubs, and gargoyles. Its 88 miles of bookshelves house over 34 million books, manuscripts, maps and prints. It is considered one of the five great research libraries of the world. Over 11,000 people enter the library on an average day.

The statues of *Beauty* and *Truth* (L-R of the entrance) are by Frederick MacMonnies. Paul Bartlett designed the 11-foot-high figures on the frieze of (L-R) *History, Drama, Poetry, Religion* and *Romance.* The celebrated lions are by Edward Clark Potter. Their original names were *Lady Astor* and *Lord Lenox.* Mayor La Guardia renamed them *Patience* and *Fortitude.*

National Historical Landmark 1966. N.Y.C. Landmark January 11, 1967.

WOOLWORTH BUILDING
Cathedral of commerce
233 BROADWAY, AT BARCLAY STREET

The Woolworth Building opened on April 24, 1913 when President Wilson pressed a button in Washington, D.C., illuminating its 80,000 lights. The building was the predecessor of the skyscrapers of the 1920s that transformed New York City's skyline. Designed in the *Gothic Revival* style, it took three years to build and the construction cost of $13.5 million was paid for in cash.

Frank Winfield Woolworth, *Merchant.* After his first five-cent store failed in Utica, Ny., Woolworth opened a five-and-ten-cent store in Lancaster, Pa. in 1879. Within 32 years, he had established a chain of over 1,000 stores. The F. W. Woolworth Company still owns and operates from the building.

Cass Gilbert, *Architect.* Also designed the U.S. Custom House and U.S. Court House in New York and the Supreme Court Building in Washington, D.C.

The 60-story building consists of a 30-story base and a 30-story tower capped by a copper-clad pyramidal roof. Rising to a height of 792 feet, it was the tallest skyscraper for seventeen years until the Chrysler Building was completed in 1929. Terra cotta covers the structural steel skeleton from the fourth floor to the building's top. The vertical rows of windows rise between terra cotta-clad piers, emphasizing its verticality. The *Gothic* detailing of cream terra cotta includes flying buttresses, pinnacles, and sculptured gargoyles, beasts and masks.

The lobby features glass mosaic vaultings, stained-glass ceilings and terra cotta reliefs. The caricature reliefs of Frank Woolworth counting his nickels and dimes (inset) and Cass Gilbert studying a model of the Woolworth Building (back cover) were designed by Thomas R. Johnston.

N.Y.C. Landmark April 12, 1983.

GRAND CENTRAL TERMINAL

The noble gateway to New York
42ND STREET AND PARK AVENUE

Designed in the *Beaux-Arts* style, the terminal, a multipurpose urban center, was opened to the public in 1913. It was financed by Cornelius Vanderbilt's New York Central Railroad at a cost of $80 million.

Reed & Stem, *Architects.* St. Paul, Minnesota. Awarded the commission based on their competition-winning design. This team was responsible for the original solutions to the building's functional problems.

Warren & Wetmore, *Architects.* Responsible for the building's overall design and the *Beaux-Arts* detailing. They also designed the New York Yacht Club.

William J. Wilgus, *Engineer and Vice President of the New York Central Railroad.* Following the electrification of the trains, Wilgus was able to cover the train yards north of the terminal and utilize the air rights for real estate developments.

The terminal's steel frame construction is clad in Stony Creek granite and Bedford limestone. The 42nd Street façade has three grand arches each framed with colossal Doric columns grouped in pairs. Above the central arch is a 13-foot clock, surrounded by the sculpture of *Mercury, Hercules* and *Minerva* by Jules A. Coutan. Below is the statue of the founder of the original railroad, Commodore Cornelius Vanderbilt by Albert De Groot, 1869.

The main concourse (120 ft. W x 275 ft. L x 125 ft. H) is a thoroughfare for half a million passengers a day. It is a beautifully proportioned space designed with three full high arches that allow in streams of light from the east and west. The zodiac mural on the vaulted ceiling, by Paul Helleu, was painted in mirrored image by mistake. There are 66 tracks on the upper level and 37 tracks on the lower level.

N.Y.C. Landmark September 21, 1967.

METROPOLITAN MUSEUM OF ART

The largest art museum in the western hemisphere

FIFTH AVENUE, 80TH STREET TO 83RD STREET

This museum houses one of the most comprehensive art collections in the world with more than 3.3 million works of ancient, medieval, classical, and modern art. From its *Gothic* origins to its more recent glass walled additions, the museum reflects the major architectural styles of the last century. As the museum's art collection has grown and required more space, additions have been incorporated into the original structure.

Calvert Vaux and **Jacob Wrey Mould,** *Architects.* Designed the original Gothic building, 1874–80, which faced onto Central Park. The arcaded center portion of the west façade is the only visible remnant of the original building.

Richard Morris Hunt, *Architect.* The building's orientation to Fifth Avenue was established in 1895 when he designed the Fifth Avenue *Beaux-Arts* pavilion and Grand Hall. **Richard Howland Hunt** became *Construction Architect* after his father's death. At the main entrance three monumental arches are flanked with pairs of Corinthian columns, which support massive blocks of stone. Hunt intended the blocks to be used for sculptures, but monies were never available.

McKim, Mead & White, *Architects.* The restrained *Classical* style north and south wings on Fifth Avenue were their design, 1911–13.

Roche, Dinkleloo & Associates, *Architects.* Designed the three glass walled additions, 1975–82.

Two remnants of the city's landmark buildings have been incorporated into the museum: the façade of the old Assay Office building from Wall Street, built in 1823, is part of the American Wing; and the pediment of the Madison Square Presbyterian Church, 1906, is part of the Museum Library façade.

N.Y.C. Landmark June 9, 1967. Interior Landmark November 15, 1977.

CHRYSLER BUILDING

Dedicated to world commerce and industry
405 LEXINGTON AVENUE AT 42ND STREET

The 77-story *Art Deco* style building celebrates the automobile as well as the modern skyscraper. In 1929 it became the world's tallest building when architect William Van Alen secretly had the 185-foot spire assembled in the dome and then added to the 925-foot tall building. The Chrysler Building thus surpassed the just completed Bank of Manhattan's height of 927 feet which was designed by his former partner and rival, H. Craig Severance. Its fame as the world's tallest building was short lived, however, as the Empire State Building was completed 18 months later.

Walter P. Chrysler, *Automobile Industrialist.* Founder and president of the Chrysler Automobile Corporation.

William Van Alen, *Architect.*

Constructed of a white ceramic brick with stainless steel ornamentation, the Chrysler Building was one of the first to use stainless steel as a building material. The fourth setback (26th floor) is adorned with white and grey brick automobile patterns and is capped-off at each corner with ten-foot-high winged radiator caps (inset). At the fifth setback, eight stainless steel eagle gargoyles perch over the edge.

Although Van Alen's architectural plan specified lighting the tower of stainless steel arches and triangular windows, it was not illuminated until 1981.

The angular lobby consists of multicolored marble and granite; a ceiling mural by Edward Trumball, depicting the Chrysler Building, transportation and industry; and elevator doors and walls decorated with stylized floral designs of exotic inlaid woods.

N.Y.C. Landmark September 12 1978.

The Empire State Building

The cathedral of the skies

350 Fifth Avenue

The Empire State Building was the world's tallest skyscraper from its completion on May 31, 1931 until 1973 when the World Trade Center was built. The building's cost was $41 million, $19 million under budget. It was built in only 18 months.

Shreve, Lamb & Harmon, *Architects.*

John J. Raskob, *Developer.* Conceived of and raised the funding for the Empire State Building at a time when the country was in financial crisis.

Alfred E. Smith, *President of the Empire State Company.* Former Governor of New York State for four terms.

Built on the site of the original Waldorf-Astoria Hotel, the building rises 1,454 feet to the top of its T.V. tower. Limestone, granite, nickel, aluminum and over ten million bricks comprise the exterior. The building's basic components, windows, stone and steel spandrels, were fabricated off site and installed as if on an assembly line. The tower rises from a five-floor base and is capped with a monumental spire. The three-story-high lobby is finished in European marble, stainless steel and glass in geometric patterns typical of the *Art Deco* period.

The Empire State Building was immortalized in the 1933 movie *King Kong*. In 1945 the building withstood the impact of a B-25 Bomber into its 79th floor. The first time the top 30 floors were illuminated was in 1977 when the N.Y. Yankees won the World Series. Since then, the tower's colors change to mark the various holidays and special events. It remains one of the most famous and revered skyscrapers in the world.

N.Y.C. Landmark May 19, 1981. National Historical Landmark October 23, 1986.

ROCKEFELLER CENTER

A city within a city

FIFTH TO SIXTH AVENUES, BETWEEN WEST 48TH TO WEST 51ST STREETS

Rockefeller Center is the world's largest privately owned business and entertainment complex. The original complex of 14 buildings on 12 acres of land was the first development where skyscrapers were designed as a group. Initially, the site was to provide a home for New York's Metropolitan Opera House. In 1929, after the stock market crash, the Metropolitan Opera withdrew from the project and the focus of the complex shifted to a mixed business center in order to avoid financial disaster. The *Art Deco* complex, built 1932–40, replaced over 200 smaller buildings in the area and employed over 75,000 workers during the Depression.

John D. Rockefeller, Jr., *Developer.*

Hood, Godley & Fouilhoux; Corbett, Harrison & MacMurray; Reinhard & Hofmeister, *Architects.* These firms worked together to design the first architecturally coordinated complex in New York City.

The centerpiece of the complex is the GE Building at 30 Rockefeller Plaza (formerly the RCA Building). The slender limestone tower rises from a four-foot granite base to a height of 850 feet. Its vertical rows of windows soar between limestone with aluminum trim for 70 stories. It is the combination of high and low buildings, gardens and plazas that creates the grandness and openness of Rockefeller Center.

Over 100 murals, mosaics and sculpture, by 39 different artists, adorn Rockefeller Center. Two of the more famous are *Prometheus,* in the Sunken Garden, and *Atlas* (inset) in front of the International Building.

The center is also the home to Radio City Music Hall, the Rainbow Room and NBC Studios. Over the years Rockefeller Center has grown and now incorporates 19 buildings on 22 acres.

N.Y.C. Landmark April 23, 1985. National Historic Landmark 1987.

RADIO CITY MUSIC HALL

Showplace of the nation

1260 AVENUE OF AMERICAS

When Radio City Music Hall opened as a vaudeville entertainment house on December 27, 1932, it was the nation's largest theater. The *Art Deco* styling combined with the grandness of its interior space celebrates a high point in American theater design.

Samuel L. "Roxy" Rothafel, *First Director of the Music Hall.* Famous for his combination of silent movies and live entertainment, Roxy was responsible for the hall's design and entertainment policies.

Donald Deskey, *Interior Designer.* Won the design commission with his stylized *Art Deco* theater design.

The grand foyer (60 ft. H x 60 ft. W) is an entire city block long. It is graced with floor to ceiling mirrors and drapes, two 29-foot-long chandeliers and a 24-carat gold leaf ceiling. *The Fountain of Youth* mural by Ezra Winter is the backdrop for the foyer's grand staircase. The 5,874-seat auditorium is dominated by the golden proscenium arches radiating from the stage. Roxy's analogy was of the sun setting on the ocean. The 144-foot-wide stage has a 43-foot diameter turntable and three cross sections that can be lowered or raised independently. The stage's hydraulic system was so innovative that the Navy studied it for its applications to aircraft carrier technology.

The world renowned precision dancers, *The Rockettes,* moved to the music hall from the Roxy Theater in 1934. The troupe began in St. Louis in 1925 as the *Sixteen Missouri Rockets* under the direction of Russell Markert. Out of a company of 60 dancers, 36 perform on stage at the music hall.

The hall has been host to premier movie showings, live stage productions, concerts, T.V. events, the Moscow Circus, the Grammy Awards, and its annual Christmas Spectacular. In 1979, the music hall's interior was restored to its 1930s design.

N.Y.C. Landmark April 23, 1985. N.Y.C. Interior Landmark March 28, 1978.

UNITED NATIONS

Promoting international peace and security

FIRST AVENUE, FROM 42ND STREET TO 48TH STREET

The United Nations complex of three buildings; Secretariat, General Assembly and Conference Building, was designed by an international committee of 14 architects. Its 18 acres were purchased with a gift of $8.5 million from John D. Rockefeller, Jr. Built 1947 to 1953, the cost of the three buildings was approximately $67 million.

Le Corbusier (Charles-Édouard Jeanneret), *Design Architect.* France. Credited with the conceptual design for the United Nations.

Wallace K. Harrison, Harrison & Abramovitz, *Architectural Chairman and Construction Architect.* Also Director of the Board of Architects for Lincoln Center.

Trygve Halvdan Lie, *First Secretary General of the United Nations, 1946–53.*

The name "United Nations" was coined by United States President Franklin D. Roosevelt in 1941 describing the countries fighting against the Axis Powers in WW II. The name replaced the "League of Nations" that had been established by the peace treaties of WW I. In 1945 the United Nations Charter, establishing the United Nations, was drafted by its 51 original member countries.

The Secretariat is the 39-story, 544-foot-high, narrow vertical building. Completed in 1950, it was New York's first building with an all glass curtain wall; green glass set in an aluminum grid rises unbroken to the building's top. Its north and south elevations, 72 feet wide, are covered in Vermont white marble. The General Assembly is the sculptured limestone building with the concave shaped roof and central dome. The Conference Building facing the East River links the Secretariat and the General Assembly.

SOLOMON R. GUGGENHEIM MUSEUM

Let each man exercise the art he knows

1071 FIFTH AVENUE

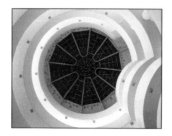

The Guggenheim is one of the city's most unique and controversial buildings. After 16 years of design and construction changes to accommodate the city's department of building codes, the museum's directors and public outcry, the museum opened in October, 1959. The building's "organic" spiral form is completely foreign to the traditional Fifth Avenue façade of aligned rectangular buildings facing out onto Central Park.

Solomon R. Guggenheim, *Copper Magnate.* Established the Solomon R. Guggenheim Foundation for his collection of non-objective art.

Baroness Hilla Rebay, *First Director of the Museum.* Under her guidance Guggenheim's art collection shifted from old masters to abstract art. She was instrumental in creating Guggenheim's art collection, the museum and in hiring Frank Lloyd Wright as architect.

Frank Lloyd Wright, *Architect.* One of America's premiere architects. The museum is his only building in New York City.

The museum's completion was also accomplished through the efforts of **Harry Guggenheim**, president of the foundation after Solomon R. Guggenheim's death in 1949 and **James J. Sweeney**, the museum's second Director.

The museum is constructed of cream colored reinforced concrete. The main gallery, an expanding spiral, is attached to the administration building, a smaller circular structure, by a concrete slab. The art is displayed along a quarter-mile-long ramp which spirals up 92 feet high to a domed skylight. The permanent art collection housed in small galleries off the ramp includes works by Klee, Kandinsky, Chagall, Robert Delaunay and Léger. Wright intended the museum's lighting to be natural from the continuous glazing ringing the outer wall and from the central skylight. However, as the natural lighting proved inconsistent, florescent lighting was later installed.

N.Y.C. Landmark August 14, 1990.

LINCOLN CENTER

For the performing arts

COLUMBUS AVENUE TO AMSTERDAM AVENUE, 62ND STREET TO 66TH STREETS

Lincoln Center, a 14-acre complex of buildings that cost a total of $185 million to construct, is dedicated to drama, music and dance. Although Lincoln Center has been criticized from the beginning by urban planners and by architects, it remains the largest, most comprehensive performing arts center in New York City. It caters to a yearly audience of five million and supports a staff of over 6,800.

Robert Moses, *New York City's Slum Clearance Administrator.* He proposed turning the area of primarily tenant row houses into a place for culture.

John D. Rockefeller, III, *Head of the Building Committee.*

Wallace K. Harrison, *Director of the Board of Architects.* Also a member of the architectural board for the United Nations and Rockefeller Center.

The buildings, surrounding an elevated plaza, are rectangular in plan, with flat roofs and colonnades and finished in white travertine marble. Their classical style and layout is often compared to an acropolis of classical antiquity.

The three principle buildings are: The **Metropolitan Opera House,** 1966, **Wallace K. Harrison** of Harrison & Abramovitz, *Architect.* Facing Broadway at the center of the plaza, the Opera House dominates the complex. Behind the ten-story-high arches and the glass wall is an interior of plush red carpets, sweeping marble stairs and a gold leaf ceiling. In the lobby are two large murals by Marc Chagall. The **New York State Theater,** 1964, **Philip C. Johnson** and **Richard Foster,** *Architects.* Located on the south side of the plaza, it is the home of the New York City Opera and the New York City Ballet. **Avery Fisher Hall,** 1962, **Max Abramovitz** of Harrison & Abramovitz, *Architect.* Home of the New York Philharmonic, it stands on the north side of the plaza. In an effort to improve the acoustics, the theater has been renovated several times. Other buildings in the complex include the Vivian Beaumont Theater, 1965; the Library and Museum of the Performing Arts, 1965; the Juilliard School of Music, 1968; and the Guggenheim Band Shell, 1969.

WORLD TRADE CENTER

The Twin Towers

CHURCH STREET, BETWEEN LIBERTY STREET AND VESSY STREET

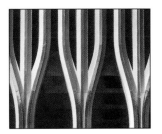

The World Trade Center was completed in 1976, after more than ten years of construction, at an estimated cost of $700 million. It is the world's second tallest building. The Sears Tower in Chicago is the tallest.

Minoru Yamasaki, *Design Architect.*

Emery Roth & Sons, *Construction Architects.*

Port Authority of New York and New Jersey, *Financiers and Builders.*
The complex is owned and operated by the Port Authority.

The twin towers include a number of architectural innovations such as load bearing exterior piers (similar to the masonry buildings of the late 19th century), providing column-free floor space, and sky lobbies, where express elevators meet with local elevators. The external piers form *Neo-Gothic* arches at the ground level and the 107th floor, a gesture to the classic base, shaft and capitol divisions.

The World Trade Center is the world's largest commercial complex. Built on landfill reclaimed from the Hudson River, it covers an area of over 16 acres and includes two 110-story stainless steel and glass towers, each a quarter-mile high; as well as three low-rise plaza buildings and a 22-story international hotel creating a completely autonomous complex. The ten million square feet of office space holds 50,000 working people and an additional 80,000 visitors a day.

A five-acre plaza links the complex of buildings. In the center of the plaza the 25-foot-high bronze revolving *Globe,* by Fritz Koenig, sits atop a black granite fountain. Below the plaza are six levels containing shops, restaurants, PATH and subway lines and parking for over 2,000 automobiles.

BIBLIOGRAPHY

A FEW OF THE PRIMARY SOURCES USED FOR RESEARCHING
THE ARCHITECTURE AND HISTORY OF NEW YORK CITY:

The Landmarks of New York
Barbaralee Diamonstein

Blue Guide New York
Carol von Pressentin Wright

The Architecture of New York City
Donald Martin Reynolds

The WPA Guide to New York City
Federal Writers Project, 1930

New York 1900
R. A. Stern, G. Gilmartin, J. Massengale

New York 1930
R. A. Stern, G. Gilmartin, T. Mellins

The Skyscraper
Paul Goldberger

AIA Guide to New York City
Elliot Willensky & Norval White

New York, A Guide to the Metropolis
Gerard R. Wolfe

History Preserved, A Guide to New York City
Landmarks and Historic Districts
Harmon Goldstone & Martha Dalrymple

Copyright © 1991 by Charles J. Ziga

All rights reserved. No part of this book may be reproduced or transmitted
in any form or by any means, electronic or mechanical, including
photocopying, recording, or by any information storage and retrieval system,
without permission in writing from the Author.

Inset photograph on page 58 copyright © 1988 by David Heald, courtesy of
the Solomon R. Guggenheim Museum.

This edition published by Barnes & Noble Inc.
by arrangement with Charles J. Ziga, Ziga Design.

1991 Barnes & Noble Books

ISBN 0-88029-717-4

Printed and bound in the United States
M 9 8 7 6 5 4 3 2 1